Introduction to Internet

Credit Card Theft, Work-At-Home

Dueep J. Singh

Mendon Cottage Books

JD-Biz Publishing

Disclaimer

The information is this book is provided for informational purposes only. It is not intended to be used and medical advice or a substitute for proper medical treatment by a qualified health care provider. The information is believed to be accurate as presented based on research by the author.

The contents have not been evaluated by the U.S. Food and Drug Administration or any other Government or Health Organization and the contents in this book are not to be used to treat cure or prevent disease.

The author or publisher is not responsible for the use or safety of any diet, procedure or treatment mentioned in this book. The author or publisher is not responsible for errors or omissions that may exist.

Warning

The Book is for informational purposes only and before taking on any diet, treatment or medical procedure, it is recommended to consult with your primary health care provider.

Our books are available at

1. Amazon.com
2. Barnes and Noble
3. Itunes
4. Kobo
5. Smashwords
6. Google Play Books

Table of Contents

Getting to Know More about Internet Scams/Identity Theft/Credit Card Theft and Internet Frauds

Introduction to Internet Scams and Frauds

With the Internet becoming such an integral part of all our lives, is it a surprise that we are more vulnerable to Internet scams and Internet fraud. So for all those people who want to know about the different ways in which a person can get scammed through Internet scams and Internet fraud, here is a complete information dossier telling you all about identity thefts, credit card thefts, Internet fraud and Internet scams.

Along with this, you are going to know more about how fraudsters can gain access to your bank account, thanks to emails which you demand information from you under the garb of updating your banking details and information.

Ignorance is not bliss. In such cases you have to be one step ahead of all the scamsters who benefit from a credulous public who believe that if banking and financial company officials have written to you about a serious matter, it is serious. They thrive on such threatening and scare tactics, telling you that your account is going to be limited within three days or some such ultimatum.

Remember that no bank or any other institution which has anything to do with money is going to ask you for your details, by asking you to update them online. Anybody with a little bit of common sense knows that any information which is sent online either through mail or through tapping on supposedly secure websites can be easily accessed by any hacker with a little bit of experience and computer know how.

So apart from showing you ways and means with which you can check these Internet scamsters and credit card identity thieves, this book is going to give you information on how you can protect yourself from future financial losses.

Difference between Internet scams And Internet Fraud

Internet scams can be you telling the details of your credit card or your identity to companies who demanded this information from you, because they need that information to see whether you are of age or any other excuse.

Internet fraud is much more of the same thing, but on a larger level with transactions through companies sending money through wire transfers to other companies abroad. These companies do not exist.

Tips and Techniques to Recognize Frauds and Scams

Rule number one – giving personal information out

Common sense is not so common, but you should have some survival instinct working, especially when somebody is demanding to know your name, address, phone number, and other important information, because they need it. No legitimate business needs this information from you, especially over the Internet.

Also, anybody asking for your credit card details, unless of course it is eBay or any other such site should also be considered to be a pukka SCAM. It is better to be safe than to be sorry. Once you lose your money, you are never going to get it back. Somebody is going to be making his own bungalow in some South American country through money stolen from you.

So remember any site page on the Internet which asks you to give your personal details, especially password, name, address, phone number, and bank account number is a scamster.

Rule number two – identification documents

In fact, any company out there has absolutely no right to ask you for identification documents, including your passport details to prove you are who you are. While I was working for Odesk they told me to verify my identity for their files. They wanted my passport details. I kicked up a fuss. They had absolutely no right to ask me my passport details, or my national identity card details or my income tax number details, or even my bank account proof details.

And I received a letter from them saying *that a technical fault had caused a sending of mail requiring proof to all their clients/customers/contractors.* My account was immediately reopened again. They had suspended it, thanks to their technical blooper.

But how many of the clients in Asia, and the Middle East and in other parts of the world sent their passport details to Odesk in order to prove their identity?

One may trust Odesk, to keep that information confidential but one definitely should not trust the medium by which you send those documents – a Hotmail or a Google mail or a yahoo mail server. This is one of the easiest things to hack online, and any teenage geek with a little bit of slick techno- know how can get access to millions of email addresses with a couple of clicks of his fingers on his mouse.

These email addresses can be dispersed all over the world to be used by fraudsters. As for your documents, they can be accessed by anybody – read government or nongovernment agency, i.e. Microsoft, anywhere in the world and tabulated in the dossier are being built against you, by some nosy Parker, who has nothing else to do!

Talk about big Brother paranoia, but one does feel this way, especially when there is absolutely no safety on the Internet, and no recourse to any sort of identity Theft and credit card theft.

How does Internet fraud work?

You have to be very careful, to see if something is a scam or not. Scamming is one of the most common ways in which people get money from you, and like I said you never get it back again.

This can happen in a number of ways. You give your personal details to people who demanded from you, pretending to be either people from your bank or from some website, which promises to keep your details secure.

Rule number one of protecting yourself from Internet scams and Internet frauds.

This is for all those people who are completely thrilled when they find themselves getting messages that they have USD1 million in some Spanish lottery or Marcus Zuckerman has chosen their name out of Facebook and decided to present them with USD1 million or some well-known agency somewhere abroad wants you to update your details, because you forgot to do so in the first place.

Let me give you an example. I have been using PayPal for a long time for all my transactions abroad. My clients abroad pay me through PayPal. The best thing is that the Reserve Bank of India has made sure that all the money coming from abroad is going to go straight into my official bank account somewhere here in India. That means I cannot get away, especially when I have to pay my income tax!

Also, I cannot pay for purchases abroad, through the money earned from abroad, and going back abroad. All of us Indian users of PayPal – I defy anybody to say you did not do this – did this until Reserve Bank of India got wise!

That is why there are so many people out there who know that they cannot get money from us in our PayPal accounts. But they would want to hack our passwords, would not they to see how much money is coming in?

So that is why they are going to send you an email like the one given below. This is going to go straight in your junk box, because it is a scam. If it was a genuine letter from PayPal, it would have gone straight into your inbox. It would have been addressed to you with your name written clearly. It would have your email address on it.

A scam mail does not have your email address. It does not have your name written on it, though, scammers are getting to be cleverer and are going to write your name, sometimes. So you think that it is a genuine mail from your client or service provider or bank.

No financial company in the world today asks for your details on the Internet. Or on the phone. Remember that. This includes banks.

So look out for this scam in your junk mail. This is being sent by the millions every day by scammers all over the world to trap simple trusting souls like you and me.

Example 1.
Your Account PayPal Has Been Limited !
Your Account PayPal Has Been Limited !
Actions
Service-PayPal (paypal@cliient.com)
Add to contacts
21-11-2014
To:

From: **Service-PayPal** (paypal@cliient.com) Your junk email filter is set to exclusive.
Sent: 21 November 2014 20:16PM
To:
This message is here because your junk email filter is set to exclusive.
Wait, it's safe!|I'm not sure. Let me check
PayPal

Dear member:
Das part of our security measures, We regularly monitor the activities taking place in the PayPal system. We recently contacted following a

problem with your PayPal account.

Information you have requested for the following reason :

Our system has detected unusual rates on a credit card associated with your PayPal account.

File #: PP-1124-075-998

This is a final reminder asking you to log in to PayPal as soon as possible.

Please restore access to your account.

Please do not reply to this email. Emails sent to this address can not be answered.

This is a very dangerous scam of the first order. It is being sent all over the world, to millions of email addresses. Some of these addresses **do not even have a PayPal account!** Others who have been using PayPal for a number of financial transactions are going to get extremely worried, because they think that there is a problem with their account.

So what do you do under such circumstances?

Look very carefully – where is your email address? Where is your name? If this was a genuine message sent to you from PayPal, you would have found it on the PayPal notification board when you logged in on to the site. Instead, this scam has used the generation term "member." And "customer."

Then look at the quality of the language in the letter sent to you.

Your Account PayPal Has Been Limited !

As far as I know one uses prepositions while writing letters. Where is the "on" before PayPal?

Now look very carefully at the email address of the person who has sent this to you.

Service-PayPal (paypal@cliient.com)

He cannot spell client. The.com address should have been PayPal.com. This mail screams SCAM.

The bad grammar and typos show that this letter has been sent by somebody who is extremely careless and could not bother much about rechecking the mail. That is because he is sending this mail wholesale

Das part of our security measures, We regularly monitor the activities taking place in the PayPal system. We recently contacted following a problem with your PayPal account.

Our system has detected unusual rates on a credit card associated with your PayPal account.

File #: PP-1124-075-998

Looks like this message has been written by somebody for whom English is not a native language. Also he did not study English at school, so he does not know of what he writes.

Besides this, he has used a little bit of legalese language, by giving me an authentic looking file number. So I think that I am dealing with some and dedicated PayPal employee. The number is to show him from which credit card to steal, the moment I press on the **please restore access to your account** button.

This is a final reminder asking you to log in to PayPal as soon as possible.

This is the threatening part to make you feel tense. "Oh heavens," you say to yourself "somebody is trying something nasty on my PayPal account I need to safeguard it immediately." Well, he has not done that yet. But he is

going to do exactly that, the moment you do the most logical – according to you, – but hazardous thing ever.

That is- press on this button. This button is there in your email message. Instead of doing the sensible thing and logging into your PayPal account directly from a Google server, 99 out of 100 people are going to press this button.

Please restore access to your account.

That is that. You are going to be rerouted to a scam or fraud page, which looks like your PayPal page. It has been made by expert hackers. You will be asked to login with your PayPal name and with your PayPal password.

Before you can say, hey presto, some scammer sitting 2000 miles away is going to be strewing rose is out of his hat because he has immediate access to all your information, including your credit card information and other private details which you put on PayPal. In fact, you have opened the way for identity theft by your own hand, by pressing on the button down below.

Please restore access to your account.

By the time you wake up and feel that there is something wrong, log into your PayPal account and change your password, it will be too late. These scammers work superfast. All your details are already logged in on some computer in some remote corner of the world.

So remember that if you want to open yourself up to Internet fraud, spend a lot of time opening up such fraudulent messages supposedly coming from your bank, or from your credit card division asking you to update your details.

No bank is ever going to do that. They know that the security measures on Hotmail, Google mail, Yahoo and other mail servers are pitiful and as full of leaky holes as a sieve. But as the world is made up of a large majority of stubborn fools who are not going to believe that any information passed on the Internet through mail is easily accessible by anybody who has a little bit of knowledge of computers and some hacking skills, we still continue to leave ourselves open to identity thefts.

Example number 2

Your PayPal Account Has Been Temporarily Locked !

Your PayPal Account Has Been Temporarily Locked !

Actions

PayPal Inc (paypal@support.com)

Add to contacts

06:08AM

To: **They had my email address here, which means that Paypal security has been compromised. On the other hand, it could be just a chance, using a number of hacked email addresses. One gets nervous and clicks the DANGEROUS button, below in the mail.**

From: **PayPal Inc** (paypal@support.com) Microsoft SmartScreen classified this message as junk.

Sent: 02 December 2014 06:08AM

To:

Character set: | Auto Select   ▼ |

Microsoft SmartScreen marked this message as junk and we'll delete it after ten days.

Wait, it's safe!|I'm not sure. Let me check

Notice of Policy Updates

Dear Customer, (Paypal will Never send you an email. If they do so, the email will be with your name on it.)

Some information on your account appears to be missing or incorrect.
Please update your information promptly so that you can continue to enjoy
all the benefits of your PayPal account.
If you don't update your information within 3 days, we'll limit what you can do with your PayPal account.

`update`

NEVER EVER press this button. You will immediately be rerouted to a page which looks like the original PayPal page, but has been made by fraudsters.

If you need help logging in, go to our Help Center by clicking the Help link located in the upper right-hand corner of any PayPal page.
.
Sincerely,

PayPal

Please do not reply to this email. We are unable to respond to inquiries sent to this address. For immediate answers to your questions, visit our Help Center by clicking "Help" at the top of any PayPal page.

Of course they are asking you not to reply to this email. If you had done so PayPal would have been inundated with inquiries from authentic customers asking the reason why this mail had been sent to them in the first place.

Lottery Scams

If you are new to Hotmail or to any other mail server, and have just looked into your junk box, it is possible that you are going to be thrilled by messages telling you that your Internet email address has won USD1 million.

Oh wow, you scream with joy. But you are not going to ask yourself some basic things —Are these guys your dear cherished uncles from abroad who are giving away money to you free, because they have no better thing to do, except keep pulling out email addresses out of a hat and informing them that they have won USD1 million? Well, they are trying to make a Klutz out of you.

Prize draw , sweepstake and lottery frauds are going to happen when fraudsters contact you through email, and tell you that you have won a really used amount of money through an international sweepstake, lottery or prize draw.

It does not matter that you do not know anything about such a sweepstake because you belong to a country far far away from Canada, Australia or Spain, where the sweepstakes take place. Also, you did not buy a ticket, but hey, you won millions and millions of crisp notes. This is a European lottery, but the agent is living in Lagos, Nigeria.

How many times have you used your email address to buy a lottery, if you have ever bought one? Think it over. However, people still fall for the "your email address was selected" scam.

After this, you are going to be asked to contact somebody who is going to be a high-ranking official of the sweepstake or lottery company. This message is also going to tell you not to spread the good word around. This in itself should show you that this is a scam. If it was a genuine sweepstake, and you had really held the winning ticket as proof, there would be camera persons camped out at your doorstep, asking such puerile questions like you have won USD1 million, how does it feel like. And let us see your face, and smile, please, face the camera you have won USD1 million, what does it feel like.

A genuine sweepstake is going to thrive on publicity and get the most of it. It is going to bring with it the media in every form, shape, size and color. You are going to be hounded for the rest of your life by publicity hunters, people wanting your autograph or a free handout. You are going to find long-lost relatives coming out of the woodwork, giving free interviews to the media that you are their favorite nephew and you loved your very loving aunt so much who treated you like a mother when you were a child.

However, a scam is always going to tell you not to tell anybody about your good fortune. Oh, really?

Some of these fraudsters send you an email, after a sweepstake has been announced by a genuine lottery. Congratulations, you are a winner.

Use your common sense. You have not won any money because either the lottery company does not exist or it has been using the identity of a genuine well-known lottery. There is absolutely no prize money coming to you.

Now, here comes the clever part where they are going to ask you for proof of identity. This includes giving information about your passport, to show you that you are the genuine Mr. A.N.Onimuss.

Here is a scam from Google. You may also get Coca-Cola scams, Microsoft scams, and even FBI giving away money to your email address! **Please you are advised not to complete the form below!**

Please you are advised to complete the form below and send it immediately to our Claims Administrator through email or fax for prompt collection of your winning fund.

The Claims Administrator Google Promotion Award Team.

Mr. Trevor Allan
Google Promotion Award Team
Email: trevorallan_googleuk@live.co.uk
Phone: +447017031320

You are advised to contact your Claims Administrator with the following details to avoid unnecessary delay and complications:

PAYMENT PROCESSING DETAILS/FORM.
(1) Your complete contact address:
(2) Your Tel/Mobile numbers:
(3) Your Nationality/Country:
(4) Your Full Name:
(5) Occupation/Company:
(6) Age/Gender:
(7) Have you ever won an online lottery?
(8) What is your comment on Google Product and services?
(9) Alternative email account if any:

So you are hereby strongly advised once more to keep your winnings strictly confidential until you claim your prize.

Congratulations from the Staffs & Members of the Google interactive Lotteries Board Commission.

Sincerely,
Dr. Leslie Spears.
Google Promotion Award Notification Dept.

If you supply them with other details like your passport number, you are letting yourself open to Internet fraud of the first order, including future identity theft. Besides, "Google" is telling you to keep your winning strictly confidential.

Remember that no big company out there, including Microsoft, Facebook, Google, or any other well-known company is running any sort of lottery. Unfortunately, they cannot prevent the scamsters from using their names for cheating and scamming other people on the Internet.

The moment you respond to them, you are going to be asked to pay a large amount of money, which is going to include banking fees, taxes, legal fees, and money transfer fees, etc. many of us think, all right, we are going to be getting so much money, so this little amount is all right. Let us pay it. After you make your first payment, you are going to be sent another message that there was some sort of hitch in the proceedings and you will need to send some more money before they can release the winnings which are nonexistent and which have been coloring your imagination Golden and pink with hope for the past couple of days.

Also, you are going to get some supposedly justified reason why they cannot take this money out of your winnings, but it has to be paid up front. And you had better give them your banking details because the money is going to be paid directly straight into your account.

The moment you hand over this confidential information to them, there goes your banking balance, and all your hard-earned money emptied out and now sent to a bank somewhere in Lagos or Nigeria.

Victim of Lottery Fraud?

So what do you do if you manage to become a victim of lottery fraud?

You can only become a victim of lottery fraud, **if you responded** to that official looking letter telling you that you have won a huge amount of money. After that you paid some fees, so that your winnings could be released to you.

What do you do under such circumstances?

Unfortunately, many of us do not have any recourse to victims of lottery fraud. Go online, and you are going to see a number of people all over the world, who are posting on forums, because either they have been victims of this fraud, and they are asking for help to get their money back. Or they have been sensible and are telling the rest of the world that such scams are frauds.

If you have already responded to such a message, make sure that you go to your bank and tell them that you have sent some supposed scamsters your bank details, and they need to be on the lookout. If you are fortunate enough to be banking with banks, which have a laissez-faire attitude, the fraudster is going to have ample time to empty out your account, before the officials wake up and take any action. [More information about this is given below in **how banks are helping to encourage Internet scam and fraud**.]

The sad thing is that once you have fallen victim to an Internet fraud, another vulture is out there ready to pick your bones. He is going to come in the shape of a law enforcement officer, or a lawyer, willing to help you get your money back. And he is going to ask for payment for his services. You, in desperation are going to hire him. He is going to go laughing all the way to his bank, while you find yourself sitting on a bank account which says UK pound 0.00 balance, or US dollars 0.00 balance...

Giving Money Away Free Scam

This comes under the category of a begging letter. Thanks to the Iraq war, you are going to get plenty of letters from people supposedly highly connected with Saddam Hussein, and trying desperately hard to get their funds out of Iraq, with a little bit of help from you. Or you may get some message from somebody in Syria, or somewhere else in Russia or in the Middle East because these are the politically disturbed hotspots globally at the moment.

For this effort, you are going to receive a percentage. They just want your details so that they can contact you further. Give your details and then spend the rest of your life worrying about identity theft.

I remember a letter being sent to me, about 10 years ago from a person in the Middle East. He supposedly suffered from cancer. He wanted to give his money away because his family members were greedy. And he wanted my help to help disburse that money.

Of course that was a general letter sent all over the world, but I was in a half sleepy mood and I answered back that I really did not have the time and energy to help him disburse his money, but he could manage to bear the pain of the cancer by drinking a steeped strong and concentrated potion of red clover flowers. That would help him die easier because he was in the last stages and I could not help him anymore.

Well, that was the only letter I wrote back to one of these scammers. However, I forgot one thing. I had responded back, even if they did not have any of my personal details. **They had my email address. After that, I was personally bombarded with more than 50 scam mails per day until I changed my email address.**

Dear friend,

Its been quite long since we heard from each other. Betrayal they say is the willful slaughter of hope. I have betrayed you my friend from the moment you responded to that email I sent to you some time ago., from that moment you accepted that lotto wining notice and then you sent me your name, address phone and account details.

From that moment I choose to betray you when you choose to trust me.I diverted the wining to myself.I am so so sorry that you have lost a lot of money to claim this prize.

I am in a poor state of health now and i may have died from cancer before my Son send you this letter,but please accept the Seven hundred and sixty thousand dollars compensation as an attonement for my sin against you.Please contact my legal adviser Barr.charles based in Malaysia because I have given him instructions to deliver this money to you as soon as possible.

You can contact my legal adviser Barr.charles his email [@lawyer.com] just tell him that you are contacting him under instruction from Code:GUMTU992 he will honor my WILL and pay you within Fourth eight hours. Forgive me this is all i ask for.Please send him your I.D,phone and address for verification and payment processing.My spirit will be uplifted once you get this compensation.

Regards
GUMTU992

This is also another example of how you are going to get a pitiful letter, playing on your emotions. Sniff, sniff. Plenty melodramatic type is not it, *I am been sore beset by people I trusted who have betrayed me* and I cannot die in peace, until you get here the money owed to you. So give me your verification and phone and address, and let me die with a content heart and atoned spirit.

Now, coming back to one particular giving away money free scam of which is the example is given below is very clever, because these rascals have set up a URL page which shows that somebody has won a lottery. He so altruistic that he is giving away USD2 million, because hey, he wants to share his good fortune with the deprived people all over the world.

And he has choose you out of the goodness of his heart to help share out these funds. This man is a confirmed lunatic trusting in the goodness of human nature, and imagining that the people who he has decided to use as ads in his global do Gooding are going to be as selfless as he is.

This in itself should show you that this is a scam.

So how do you recognize this to be a scam?

The subject line says – **Good Day**

Now, thanks to Google mail and Hotmail trapping messages which you do not have the subject written on this subject line, scammers have started writing something on the subject line. This can be hello, good day, congratulations, and even Re:

Just these few words strung together allow the mail servers to pass them on to you.

Mr. and Mrs. Bayford from UK are our great well-known philanthropists to be targeted. Look at the email address. It is not a UK email address, **but has originated in Brazil.** *La La La La La la Bra...zil* and they are brassy enough to imagine that nobody would catch them. But then most of the people they have caught would not bother to have checked the email address.

Good day,

Good day,

Actions

Mr and Mrs Bayford (direcao.graduacao@literatus.edu.br)

04:43AM

From: **Mr and Mrs Bayford** (direcao.graduacao@literatus.edu.br) Your junk email filter is set to exclusive.

Sent: 22 November 2014 04:43AM

To:

Microsoft SmartScreen has blocked this message for your safety and we'll delete it after ten days.

Show content

Good day,

I am Adrian Bayford, I and my wife were Recent winners of the euro million lottery of 148.6 GBP, and have voluntarily decided to donate the sum of 2 Million pounds (2,000,000.00GBP) to you. We have decided to use you as an aid of development in your respectful environments and we urge you that 10 percent of this donation should go to the orphanage and the less privilege.

And also you are advise to develop educational center to enhance education in your environments [now that is Spanish being literally translated into English, through Google translation...] and by doing this me and my wife could meet our goal for GLOBAL DEVELOPMENT. You are to contact Alliance Leicester Bank United Kingdom with the details below for further processing of your donation amount to your account in your country.

Visit the web pages below for more information. http://www.dailymail.co.uk/news/article-2187999/Will-148m-EuroMillions-jackpot-winner-share-fortune-long-lost-half-brother-met.html I have therefore included a Donation Code Number to this message [Bayford/231/2012ACG4] which should be kept strictly confidential as you will use it in receiving your donation.

[If you have not managed to discover that this is a scam, this is the clincher of strict confidentiality. What, a lottery winner not calling on all available media channels and radio stations to boast about his winnings and that he is giving away 2,000,000 pounds to a great hearted email address, he picked out of a hat?

But people are still falling for this scam, even today.]

You are to contact the management of ALLIANCE LEICESTER BANK PLC, UNITED KINGDOM with the code immediately as they have been authorized by me and my wife to wire the funds to you after you must have opened an account with them and concluded all process associated with the wire transfer process.
  [Again, bad Spanish translation into English. Smacks of Google translation online.]

CONTACT INFORMATION:
Customer Services Department.
Mr. Fred Powell
Address: #Aldermanbury Square,
London,EC2V Town Hall, 7SB, Hendon
London United Kingdom.
Bank E-mail: allainceleicesterb@foxmail.com

Best of luck,
Mr and Mrs Bayford

Look at the letter. These persons are supposedly based in the UK. But they cannot write proper English.

should go to the orphanage and the less privilege. And also you are advise to develop educational center.

They want me to contact one Bank email with a donation code number. That Bank email Bank E-mail: allainceleicesterb@foxmail.com is going to take me to a page where I am supposed to open up a bank account with them. For that I will need to give my details. So instead of asking my details in the email message, I am putting them online on a scamming site.

Continue reading the letter. It is very amusing with its careless spelling, sentence formation and typos.

…management of ALLIANCE LEICESTER BANK PLC, UNITED KINGDOM with the code immediately as they have been authorized by me and my wife to wire the funds to you…

Interesting, is not it, that a person supposedly based in the UK is writing a letter to you in American English? Authorized, instead of authorised?

These are some of the stupid things which trip up the scammers, so as long as you know that these people are half literate, but clever enough to catch simple people who are always dreaming of quick money, there is always going to be a fool trapped every three seconds, somewhere, somehow all over the world. Through Internet.

Stop thinking of *global development*. Instead, look to yourself, remove this message from your junk mailbox immediately and put it in your recycler. And thank your stars that you did not give out your information to these scoundrels based in Brazil.

It is a well-known fact that a lawyer in India sent seven lakh rupees [USD11,300] to one of these scammers, because he had been chosen to receive 1,000,000 UK pounds. That seven lakh rupees equivalent in pounds was supposedly for bank transfer charges and other charges needed for transferring that money. Hey, he was getting 1,000,000 pounds, so what was seven lakh rupees? Well, the papers got to know about it, and everybody in the city now knows him as seven lakh.

Talk about Some Mothers Have Them, and There Is One Born Every Moment.

This is just a pipe dream. Especially when you have not even bought the ticket!

Protecting yourself from Internet fraud

I am repeating this again and again. Nothing is free in this world. Use your common sense. If you did not buy a lottery, how could you have won it? No genuine lottery contacts people telling them that they have won. It is you who have to go and show your winning ticket to the officials to prove that you have won on the winning number.

There is absolutely no genuine lottery – state or country lottery – who asks the winner to pay for collecting his winnings. Anybody asking for any sort of payment is going to be a scam.

Never ever pay anybody anything. Never mind your family yelling at you that you have won so many million dollars, and you are such a tightwad that you cannot send USD600 to them for processing fees? Catch them by the ear and make them sit down in front of the computer. Do a Google search on the name of the lottery with the words scam attached to it. Somewhere or the other, you are going to find a hit telling you that this particular lottery is a scam.

Luckily, there are plenty of sites on the Internet, talking about lottery scams, so you may want to go through them.

Many of us humans are among the most gullible of all the people out there. The moment we hear the words dollars or pounds, we immediately say golly, one dollar is XYZ AUD, CAD, BHD, INR, etc. in today's foreign-exchange rate, so USD1 million, oh wow.

And we do not see that that particular lottery has been sent through a general Hotmail email address or a Yahoo address.

The letters are also going to be very badly written. That is because somebody wrote it out in French, or in Russian and passed it through Google translation. After it had been translated into English, through Google translation, it was transmitted to you in the form of "it is advise you" and equally bad grammar.

So the next part is going to tell you how to recognize work-at-home scams as well as how banks are helping to encourage Internet fraud and scams as well as credit card frauds, and advertisements scams.

Part 2

This portion of this book is going to be based on real life experiences, with examples and the results obtained from such examples. The bank example taken here is in India. I am sure that you have much more efficient banks in your country, wherever you are in the world. But I am just showing you the worst-case scenario of proven and inefficient bumbling and confusion, much to my regret and chagrin, as an ex-banker.

Credit card thefts/work-at-home scams/banks and scammers

Shopping online is fun, but do not give your credit card information to websites indiscriminately

In the first part of this book, we tackled Internet frauds and Internet scams. Now we come to another very important part of how fraudsters manage to get the best of us, through taking advantage of our desperation. This is the case of those people who want to work from home.

In the not so healthy global economic condition, today most of us are looking for alternative sources of income. That is why so many of us are vulnerable to these scams towards because they can promise us a regular income through just sitting at home and working as long as we have access to a computer and a fast broadband.

So this is how I am going to teach you how to recognize work from home frauds. This unfortunately is one of the ways in which many scams towards all over the world are getting rich, because people keep sending them money, hoping against hope that they are going to get a job, which is going to help make them independent, as well as help them work from home.

Work from Home Frauds – Facebook Fortune

This is the latest work-at-home fraud doing the rounds on the Internet today. They have already targeted people in the USA, UK and Philippines.

A web designer can see that this has been designed as a pop-up to load whenever you are browsing on another website. The URL has targeted the of today – Facebook. So you think it to be the genuine stuff.

Any page loading by itself is going to be a scam. This page has nothing to do with Facebook or with Mark Zuckerman. 10 years ago, it would have been Microsoft and Bill Gates. However, it has everything to do with a Ukraine or Brazil-based scamster Called Home Income Flow.

http://www.fbnewstoday.com/t3/in.html?voluu

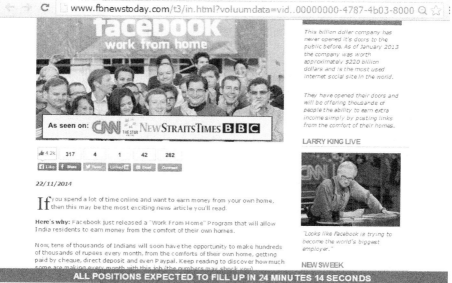

mdata=vid..00000000-4787-4b03-8000-000000000000__vpid..cb10b000-720c-11e4-84ca-59a7224b34de__caid..7ec786b2-64f1-4b1b-8eb8-8c5928020b10__lid..c10f1b2e-a9e8-4e47-98f4-ddca9b7126e5__rt..R__oid1..8acf323a-f4b2-40ca-8068-3276da0f8daa__var1..43974__var2..1&zoneid=43974&ad=1

How many of us have seen this ad? How many of us got trapped in this scam? I for one, because I did not know that the five dollars for a booklet was definitely false. USD167 were stolen from my credit card. Now you are going to ask, how did they get access to my information? When it was supposed to be free?

Here was my mistake. Even though I am an ex-banker, I was not at all instincts alert on that day. I put in my credit card details, because they wanted to confirm that I was more than 18 years old.

Country Oriented Work-At-Home Scams

So first point – never ever ever, repeat again, never put in your credit card details, however, tempting the Internet site may be. You may want to put it on eBay or on flipkart, if you are buying from their stores. But never on some site, which promises to give you information on how to work from home.

How to recognize such a scam?

So, first of all, let us see why our instincts should have begun working overtime, because this was a scam?

A page which loads by itself, when you have clicked another URL button is a scam.

This is what happened when I was browsing on another site.

If you click this URL and check it, you are going to see a number of Indian names, on Facebook telling you that they are extremely thrilled with this idea.

Scam Sign number one – a photo of an Indian with his family, telling you that he has earned so many thousand dollars through this miraculous work-at-home program.

Unfortunately, they did not tell you the name of this program until after they had stolen the money from your credit card. These rascals are a company named home income flow and they have made their millions through stealing from people in the UK and the Philippines. After that they targeted the Indians, by saying that Mark Zuckerman wanted people to work for Facebook. Before that they targeted people in the UK and the Philippines.

https://faithandalchemy.wordpress.com/2014/10/27/home-income-flow-or-facebook-fortune-all-scam/comment-page-1/

Juliet, Marian, Esther, Heidi, Asawari, Megan from the UK... All of us have been scammed, from all the corners of the world. I apologize for using your names here, wherever you are, whoever you are, but I know that you are real. I know that money has been stolen from you. And I know that you have not received any reimbursement, even though you spent days in hope. You are not going to get it back, thanks to your credit card and thanks to your bank.

MZ has plenty of other things to do other than induct Indians to work for his social networking media. He is definitely not associated with such fly-by-night scams, but many of us get caught without reading the fine print.

10 years ago, Bill Gates was being used as a front to induct people to work for his new expansion of Microsoft – work from home. Mr. Gates must have been shocked to know that he had moved away from Microsoft, and was employing them to work from home.

We are so thrilled by the idea of earning easy money that we forget the fact that there is absolutely no **company or business out there, which gives you a sure work from home guaranty.**

So if there is any company telling you that you are going to earn thousands of dollars, and you saw that they have an ad on another site, do not touch it. Unless of course you want to lose a lot of money.

Any company advertising on another site is a scam. A bona fide company is always going to have its own website with its own links. It is going to advertise its own company and you are going to get access to it on first click.

Do not press any small ad with an attractive photo of Zuckerman, promising you that he wants you to work for him. He does not.

How to Recognize a Work-At-Home Scam

Let us look at the page carefully.

It is a squeeze page, made to measure. You cannot add any information to it. This in itself should show you that this is a scam.

The English is extremely perfect. Have you seen any Facebook message, without people using SMS language or Hinglish? But here we have excellent English, in all the response messages by a number of people supposedly pasted on Facebook.

They have all their information hidden. Do you see any address or place of origin? Do you see any name of the company? It is only after you paid – without your knowledge – that you were taken to the home income flow website, which is just made up of a number of videos and absolutely nothing else.

And then you get an SMS message on your cell phone telling you that USD167 have been debited from your credit card. While you are still reeling from the shock, your next instinct is block your credit card.

And that is another headache altogether, which I am going to tackle later, especially if your bank happens to be a lethargic, inefficient bank whose employees never ever bother to stir themselves ever.

So for all those people who are looking for making quick money online, my answer is stick to your daily job. Working from home is a pipe dream. Millions of people out there may tell you, we are working from home, [I am one, but then I have my own client network, which it took 10 years to build] but for newcomers, my suggestion is – do not go in for promises that you are going to earn USD3000 per day.

The moment I found the money had been stolen away from my credit card, I went online hunting for home income flow.

Many of us update the status of this thievery on Internet forums. Asawari was diligent, but I can safely say that she may have reached the customer support and they may have promised to reimburse the money back, but she definitely would not have received it. Nor Did Megan, or Esther or Heidi.

Nor did Dueep Jyot Singh.

Any site telling you that *they are not scams* are scams. Any site telling you that they are going to reimburse your money back are thieves. Any site telling you that there is a money back guaranty if you are not hundred percent satisfied with your product – I am not just talking about programs, I am talking about any other product or service, Also, – should not be trusted.

Anti Internet Fraud agencies

On this website I got the email address of a US-based anti-Internet fraud agency on this particular URL.

https://complaint.ic3.gov/default.aspx

You can complain if you want, but you are going to get this message in return.

IC3 Complaint: I1411090429550591

IC3 Complaint: I1411090429550591

Actions

no-reply@ic3.gov (no-reply@ic3.gov)

Add to contacts

09-11-2014

Thank you for filing a complaint with the Internet Crime Complaint Center (IC3).

This is the only reply you will receive from the IC3. Because we receive thousands of complaints per week, we cannot reply to every complaint received or to every request for updates.

However, once we forward your complaint to investigators in the field, they may contact you for further information. Consequently, it is important that you maintain any evidence you have relating to your complaint. Evidence can include canceled checks, credit card receipts, phone bills, mailing envelopes, mail receipts, printed copies of websites, copies of emails, or similar items.

If you wish to view, download, or add information to your complaint, go

to http://complaint.ic3.gov/update and log in with the following:
Complaint Id: I1411090429550591
Password: CNbVBEi3Mw

To learn more about Internet schemes and ways to protect yourself
visit www.lookstoogoodtobetrue.com.

- © 2014 Microsoft

They do not seem to have enough of resources to follow-up every
complaint. But the one good thing about this No reply email is that you
have got a really good URL which you would want to look up –

www.lookstoogoodtobetrue.com

Social media advertising – YouTube etc.
Promoting Scams

So I decided to look on the Internet for how these scams were promoted. If there are some agencies all over the world, which are really interested in tackling Internet scams, they should use their sense and target the social network.

How do they catch the thief from there? Well, I am giving them the answer, and of course the thief is also going to see it, [remember 9/11 and the avid cameras broadcasting a live telecast of the commandos, in the Mumbai terrorist attack, rescuing the victims of the terrorist attack, thus giving away the positions of the commandos to the terrorists.] written here, and look for another tactic, but at least one knows which program is a scam.

Look at the work-at-home programs on YouTube. We have a home income flow video. This is a known scam. It was posted online by someone called Mark Anderson. **He had switched off comments on the video.**

This video was later removed when Youtube recognized it as a scam, thanks to my comment, which is above the video, typos included...[1]

---

[1] I wrote "US clients" as a general sweeping statement, though people in the UK and in the Philippines were also targeted by these scamsters. But every scam is tried out in the USA and Canada first, be it a lottery or a work from home scam.

+1   Add a comment...

**Major point to be noted – any video marketing any program which
promises you money sitting at home and working is a scam.** Especially
when the comments have been switched off. That is to prevent people like I
telling the rest of the world that these rogues are thieves and swindlers.

Sad to say, however much a person online is going to promise you a fixed
income through working at home, there are really not many legitimate work-
at-home programs available online.

Work-at-home programs

Many of us dream of working from home. After 18 years of piloting a desk, I decided that 9-5 jobs were a bore, especially when I had to wake up at 6:30 to get to the office by nine, through the early morning office rush.

So I decided to work-at-home.

For all those people trying to look for legitimate work-at-home gigs and sides, the answer is a disappointing well, for the last eight years, I have not found even one really bona fide and reliable work-at-home program or site which is legitimate.

You may want to try freelance jobs and gigs, but the competition is something fierce. If you are good at content writing and are based in America, UK or in Australia, you could write for TextBroker. This is good as long as you are in the USA. I got a steady income from them for about 14 months, until they put up tax related rules for USA citizens only. And by then, I was back in India and having to pay my taxes here.

You need to have your tax details at hand, for joining TextBroker.

What about freelancer.com and Elance?

I was definitely disturbed to see some people building websites for USD10 a site on Elance. Thanks to them, the quality of real professional work done by professional website designer like I has been lowered considerably. No wonder my other website designer friends in Australia, Canada, UK and the USA, and now I in India could scream. They did.

There are also places where people are willing to do jobs for you for five dollars. I just enrolled there for fun and for research purposes. In the last 1 ½ years, I have not got a single client. Have you? I will consider such sites to be wasted efforts, especially for people who want money to survive right now. They cannot afford to waste time waiting for clients to call.

Unfortunately, that is the condition of work-at-home contractors, and that is why they fall such easy prey to scams.

Many of these gigs happen to be scams. You do the work and your client disappears without paying. Luckily, I have never fallen a victim to such a thing happening to me, but I know of another freelancing friend who went instinctively to such clients! And I had to say, oh no, not again.

Tips for Working at Home Jobs

So if you want to work, freelance on Odesk-I consider this to be the most reliable of job portal providers – make sure that you have a good portfolio. Do not take up high-paying jobs, right in the beginning, when you are a newbie. Do not do free work for a client. Look at the feedback given to him. If he has no feedback, he is going to disappear because he has not been verified.

Take small jobs and get feedback. If you are serious about working from home, be sincere and dedicated. Excuses do not work in professionalism. Do not take up more than you can chew. That means that the client is not going to be satisfied with what you have done, and you are going to get a bad rating. Go the extra mile. It helps, especially in your feedback, especially if your client is very well satisfied with your work.

This feedback is going to be important to give you word-of-mouth clients were going to demand your services.

It takes about five years to get a regular network working on Odesk, working from home. I can now get my clients demanding my services, but the initial stages was rather difficult, until I got a five star rating. **It was then I threw up my well-paying tension laden stress filled, high-powered 9 to 5 job, eight years ago. [9-5 is a modest estimate. Often it was 7:30 – 8:30, seven days a week.]**

Luckily, by the time I decided to go freelance, I did not have to bother much about bills, and financial security and paying off mortgages and loans. I was working for my own pleasure on long-term jobs for people who wanted my expertise and knowledge, like web designing, translating, graphic designing etc.

All this hard-earned information had been gained through slogging on 9-5 jobs for these many long years, in most of the corners of the globe.

And now I am writing e-books, using all that hard-earned knowledge and experience, gained through all those years of study, teaching, training, learning and coaching. And I am one of the fortunate few in the world who is generating my own income, but it has been a hard road, indeed, working from home.

I would not advise you to take such a gamble, and think of working at home. When you have to generate your own income, there is no 9-5 clock watching. Even when freelancing, there were times when I had to work 8-8 for clients, who wanted the job done, like yesterday, and had given me a time bound contract, which I needed to honor because they were depending on me.

If you have a regular job, and you think that you can get a steady income through working at home, the answer is, sorry no. You may want to start freelancing, while you are working and you know that there is a regular paycheck coming in.

Do not take a chance of I will get a job online, Mr. boss, you can just go fry your face and jump in the lake. Do not do that. Jobs online are not available, however much people out there promise you that you can get them with just a click of your fingers. And if you let your regular job go, there is going to be someone out there just eager to jump in the emptied slot tomorrow morning. And there you are going to be left, high and dry with no money coming in, and the winter coming on.

Craigslist jobs are a laugh. Has anyone really got a gig through Craiglists? None that I have heard of.

How to Trap Internet tricksters Through Social Media?

This is elementary my dear Watson, but nobody's going to do that because they are too lazy. A little bit of common sense is needed here. Someone set up an account on YouTube. Someone posted that particular scam. That someone had to give his details when he was setting up a Google account.

Target those details, and get his address. A scammer is definitely not going to give his country of origin, nor his details to the rest of the world is he? But he needs to advertise on the social media network. Get the people who have posted the videos on the site, in for questioning. Someone gave them those videos. Who? At least you will get one percentage of the scams.

Now I have given you one way in which these scamsters can be stopped. Unfortunately, this method is not going to work. That is because major Internet websites are already there with plugs to prevent this information from leaking, all under the name of privacy. That is why all the major sites also happen to be one of the main reasons why all these scams are flourishing like Green Bay trees.

It is interesting to know that these sites are quite capable of giving information to government agencies like the FBI or CBI, especially in cases when persons are suspected of being terrorists. MSN has access to every single mail being sent through their servers all over the world, and have been regularly monitoring them.

So that stupid idea of privacy is obsolete and defunct. Nevertheless, if any, honest-to-goodness, real, bona fide government agency, out there, looking to prevent Internet scams and frauds goes asking the information about suspected scamsters' bona fides from Google or Hotmail or Yahoo, you are going to see the top management of these companies putting up their pious we respect the privacy of our subscribers look and you can see the scamsters scampering away, giggling.

Apart from the social media, and these major websites actively collaborating to encourage Internet scams, by being as obstructive as possible, we have some more powerful obstructionists – banks all over the world.

How Do Banks Encourage Frauds?

Banks encourage frauds? This statement is going to have a number of my banking friends baying for my blood, saying how dare you, we definitely do not encourage frauds. The answer is, my friends, do not give me that self-righteous indignant guff. I have been a banker myself. And I have seen how most of the banks work, in the East as well as in the West.

Whatever an advertising company may say, your friendly banker is friendly as long as you keep adding to your account. His job is to persuade you to keep adding to the money which you are banking with him.

I remember one really amusing joke, somewhere in the 70s. There was a cartoon of a man pointing to a sign behind a banker's head which said "**No Interest Loans**" in huge letters and the manager telling him, *yes, apart from* *our 10.25% on the loan that we are giving to you, we have no interest in you.*

There are billions hidden away in the banks all over the world, which have absolutely no heirs and nominees. Why would the bankers want to start hunting for them, and hand over that money parked by a relative so many years ago? This is the same thing for scammers.

How Can a Bank Help in Catching a Scammer?

This is a shadow exercise, but why would a bank want to do something which would cause a regular inflow of money coming in every day to be stopped? Swiss banks are banking on their reputation, which says that they do not give out the details of their clients. The real reason is that they do not intend to allow any person access to that information which is going to cause the freezing of that particular account and the possible confiscation of that money by some tax authorities somewhere else in the world.

So that moral attitude of bank with us, your money is going to be safe with us is all advertising.

That is why banks do their best to hinder any sort of activity which a client or an agency starts, which could prevent an influx of money coming in, into their banks.

This includes not giving out information about a particular clients, antecedents, which could be used as evidence and data and which would cause any sort of legal procedure which would make other clients decide to take their money away from that particular bank.

A banker has just one rule. Make sure that money stays in your bank for at least one day more, if there is a government agency breathing down your neck. And stall any investigation under any excuse. And so these investigations stretch on and on and on, while the scammers get away Scot-free.

That is because they are not going to take immediate steps ever, however much you may want, for any activity which has anything to do with a financial transaction, especially when it is money going abroad.

This includes blocking of credit cards.

Banking Laissez-faire attitudes

Example – State Bank of India Credit Card Division

Let us take the example of one of the government managed banks of India, The State Bank of India. They have been well-known to take 15 days to do a thing which should have been completed in 20 minutes. They promise you that action is going to be taken within the next five working days.

So let us take the example of the home income flow scam – starting November 9, Sunday, 2014.

I made the mistake of thinking the affiliate marketing program was free. I could cancel the program in 14 days, if I was not satisfied with it. If I was satisfied with it, I would be billed the price of the program.

Mistake number one – I did not check the billing amount. The site did not show it anywhere.

Mistake number two – I did not do an Internet research on home income flow + scam on Google. This would give me information about the scam and I would not have touched my credit card.

Dear Cardholder,
This is to inform you that,

Transaction of USD167.00 made on SBI Credit Card XXXXXX without effecting add'nl factor of authentication mandated by RBI, at AUCTION POWER ACCESS on 9 Nov 14

We hope this is in order. If not, please contact SBI Card Helpline at the earliest.
We assure you of our best service at all times.

Anyway, I was shocked when I saw a message from my SBI card notification mail telling me that USD167 had been debited from my account and I needed to tell them if it was a fraud.

It was a fraud. Someone had without my permission taken 167 dollars from my credit card. I was told in that message itself to contact helpline if that was not the case.

So I went to the SBI Visa card site and rang up the helpline.

I half expected the nasal *this nummbaar ij naat avelebul* and please check the number you have dialed. And I was not surprised when I got it.

So I wrote a letter to the contact us address at feedback@sbi.com. I was immediately presented with a mailer daemon message that this address needed to be checked.

This is an automatically generated Delivery Status Notification.

Delivery to the following recipients failed.

feedback@sbi.com

Anyway, I got an auto response on the 10th, which meant that the message was sent belatedly. This auto message told me that I would be contacted by one of their customer care people **within the next five days.**

I wanted my credit card blocked Now. Within five days, the money would have already gone into some account in Nigeria or in South America, and from there shifted to Bermuda or to Timbuktu. But could the State bank of India be bothered?Naah.

So here is a record of my trials and tribulations.

Transaction of USD 167.00 made on SBI credit card xxxxxx without affecting an additional factor of authentication mandated by RBI at AUCTION POWER ACCESS on 9 November 14.

INVALID KEYWORD – Kindly text PROBLEM to 9212500888 for us to call you back- 9 November.

10 November – your problem has reached the SBI card solution room. You will be contacted by us from phone numbers starting from 0124 or 044 within two working days. [I received the call on the 17th. That entails two working days for this bank.]

I received an email message on the 12th. Here it is.

Actions

feedback@sbicard.com

Add to contacts

12-11-2014

To: my email address

12/11/2014

Dear….

Thank you for writing to SBI Cards.

This is with reference to your communication dated 9/11/2014.

Transaction Details: We would like to inform you that as per our records, the transaction dated 9/11/2014 for Rs.10710.40, has not yet been confirmed by the concerned merchant.

Furthermore, we hereby inform you that the transactions gets cancelled automatically, in case the same is not confirmed within 21 days from the date of debit.

We would also like to request you that in case the above mention transaction get confirmed. You may raise the dispute for same.

Please advise us further course of action.

In case of any query , would request you to reply at feedback@sbicard.com using the same subject line or contact the SBI Card helpline at 39 02 02 02 or 1860 180 1290 (if calling from MTNL and BSNL lines) . IVR & Emergency Services on helpline are available 24 hours and Customer Service representatives are available from Monday to Saturday between 8am to 8pm.

If you are not satisfied with the response, you can write to Nodal Officer, Customer Service at Nodalofficer@sbicard.com using the same subject line. You will receive a response within 8 working days.

Yours sincerely,
.... - Customer Service

[THREAD ID:1-E6L0HJ]

According to it you can clearly see that the credit card thief had not asked for the transaction to go through till date. I breathed a sigh of relief and wrote back that it was a fraud, and credit card theft. So my card needed to be blocked.

On the 17th I finally got a call from the customer care service.

Dear cardholder, as per your request, we have blocked your SBI card ending xxxx SBI cards- 17 November.

Did you notice the time taken to block a card? *9 November to 17 November.* That was enough for the money to be transferred into a fraudster's bank account. *And it was transferred on the 12th November even though I had been assured that*

Transaction Details: We would like to inform you that as per our records, the transaction dated 9/11/2014 for INR.10710.40, has not yet been confirmed by the concerned merchant.

The customer care service employee *wished to inform me that the transaction had already GONE through,* and she did. She also said that she had filled in a dispute form, and she further wished to inform me that it would take 120 days for the dispute to be settled.

This would not have taken place if the money had not been shifted in the first place and my card blocked on the ninth. But thanks to the collaboration of the bankers with not so alert credit card issuers, the money was sent to a fraudster's account abroad.

Notice, that the email message on the 13 said very clearly that the money had not been shifted. That is because the client had not asked for it. This was misinformation, which was the banker's way of getting through the day and let tomorrow look for itself and that will be somebody else's problem. But the money had already been shifted on the 12th.

On 18 November I received another message from these totally muddled and confused banking professionals.

Dear SBI cardholder. This is regarding your query reference number 0133213487577 related to transaction not done. To process the same, kindly share the duly filled dispute form downloadable from sbicard.com and mail it to us at chargeback sbicard.com. Please ignore if already sent- 18 November.

The problem with these bankers is that they do not read. Or they cannot read or understand English. The dispute problem, which they brought onto themselves was because a transaction had been done. They were now confusing me with the fraudulent client, wanting to know why money had not been sent to my account.

On 22nd November I received this message.

Dear Cardholder, we are unable to establish a contact with you regarding the SMS problem. Please call our helpline at 39020202, [*This nambaar dujj naat exhist. Pleej chack da numbaar you have dialed.*] or 186-01-8010, to resolve your queries/complaint at the earliest.

I did not call them up after I got the computerized guff of checking the number I had dialed. They did not know what was going on, and I did not want to talk with another female who wished to inform me that...

[Incidentally,for all those people who have heard customer service care people and telecallers using these words ever so often, you will have to blame it on me. Yes, literally speaking, and not figuratively speaking. I was that human being who taught this trick to trainee bankers and telecallers. These were time wasting catchwords and phrases during training sessions, way back in the 90s. I did not know that this part of my banking training sessions, I had thought up would become such a universal headache entirely call centers and banks within the next 20 years.

I was also shocked to see that they were part of banking letters, sent to clients, where the bankers wished to inform me that something particularly nasty had occurred, thanks to their carelessness and laissez-faire attitude.

Some of these phrases were – *we would wish to inform you, I would like you to know that, I am happy to inform you, you would be glad to know,* and so on. These phrases were ways and means in which you could keep your mouth occupied while your mind worked by the speed of lightning, to either find a solution or to stop a client from complaining.

It also showed that I was more professional and experienced than he was. This is a superior patronizing tactic taught to all us Management professionals, in the 80s, as marketing tactics. And they are now alas universal.]

On 22nd November I received another message saying **dear cardholder, we are processing your query reference number 013213487577, relating to transaction not occurred. Thank you for your patience.**

My card was supposedly blocked on the 17 th. On the 22nd they were still worrying about **a transaction not having occurred** when it had already occurred on the 12th. And that was the main problem.

On 26 November I received a message saying – we wish to inform you that your complaint reference 0133213487577 has been resolved.

How was that resolved? Nobody knows. Finally somebody woke up to the fact that a transaction had occurred, which I was calling a fraud and a scam. So they needed to save face quickly.

On 28th I received this email –

Interaction Id-1-898069195 PreviousmessageNext messageBack to messages [InteractionId:1-857584567] Eme

Actions

Nodalofficer@sbicard.com (Nodalofficer@sbicard.com)

28-11-2014

Warm Greetings for the day!

We sincerely regret for the inconvenience caused to you on the matter addressed to us. We are committed to resolve the matter to your satisfaction.

We truly value you as our privileged customer and regret the inconvenience cause to you in the matter addressed to us. Please accept our sincere apologies for any inconvenience caused to you and for your displeasure whilst you felt our service levels did not meet your expectations. We solicit your continued patronage to our services.

We would like to inform you that your SBI Card is inactive for usage and the outstanding is Rs ....

We would like to inform you that we have taken your request for Transaction dispute of Rs. 10,699.97 towards the merchant name AUCTION POWER ACCESS and wish to assure you that we have initiated necessary investigation towards the same. [**How we Asians love red tapism. Especially through generating more work when a little bit of efficiency in the first place would not have caused all this hassle at all.**]

Please note that the maximum time for closure of such disputes is 120 days, as we are dependent on external feedback such as acquiring banker. While we try to do our best to resolve the dispute at the earliest, we request you to bear with us in the interim.

We request you to take note of the following important points:

a) All transaction disputes are resolved as per the VISA/MasterCard guidelines. We will keep you updated on the status of this dispute as well as any further requirements.

b) The dispute will be settled post completion of the investigation. In case of resolution of the dispute in favour of the cardholder, any charges levied on the disputed transaction during the period of investigation will be reversed.

Please suggest us if you want to have a new card re-issued with different card number. [I must admire the sheer effrontery of this suggestion.]

We would also hereby inform you that a replacement fee of Rs.100.00 plus government service tax (as per applicable charges) would be applicable towards the reissue / replacement of new card.

Here is the clincher –

We would like to inform you that we have given temporary credit of Rs. 10,699.97 towards the disputed transactions incurred on your card account and the same would reflect vide your statement dated December 09, 2014.

We wish to inform you that post confirmation from the merchant; same will be credited permanently on your card account.

Do you know what it means?

It means even if the money has been stolen away from the credit card, it *is going to be debited from your bank account* because after all they want their cut. And when they get confirmation from the merchant, the money is going to be credited permanently on my card account, whatever that means.

That means that they want to assure me that they are capable of catching a fly by night elusive chimera who has eluded their grasp, in 120 days. Do not make me laugh.

I would not be surprised if the dispute investigation officials know where the money has gone. That money is going to be credited back to your card in 120 days. Until then, the particular bank, which holds that account is going to enjoy the interest on it for 120 days. You may think that that interest is a trifling amount. But, Multiply 167 dollars innumerable times, and the interest itself is going to be mighty high.

Nevertheless, I took immediate steps so that they did not automatically debit that amount of money from my bank account. I cleared out my bank account and transferred the money to another account. That was once better than closing this account altogether because the credit card guys had access to its details.

You may want to do that too, if you have your bankers going in for auto debit directly from your bank account.

Continuation of that smarmy letter –

We would like to thank you for your valuable time and inputs. Such suggestions are of great importance to us, as they provide us the reason to improve our services. Your feedback would certainly enable us to provide better services to our customers.

Please feel free to contact us should you require any further assistance or clarification.

Yours sincerely,

. . . .
From Nodal Desk – SBI Card

[All these letters have been suitably edited, so that the customer care employee does not get into hot water. But the details are original and undisturbed. So is the language.]

Strict Ways of Tackling Credit Card Frauds

You mean you are suffering from a credit card fraud? Well, contact us after 120 days. We may have some news for you, by then, but do not keep your fingers crossed.

Now anybody who has gone through the ordeal of such inept bumbling will definitely understand that banks are not capable of taking instant decisions like blocking cards immediately. And after that, they get their dispute departments to go hunting for the account in which that money was sent.

Then they have to go and talk to their counterparts in that other country, telling them that that money has been stolen.

And the counterpart is going to put up a block. He does not want that money going out of his bank.

This is the excuse under which banks all over the world are operating and do not wish to give out information about their criminal clients to government agencies or to other banks all over the world.

So he is going to shout – privacy laws. He is also going to say that the rules and regulations of his bank do not permit him to give any sort of help in exchange of confidential information about a client. This client is getting USD167 regularly every day, from different credit cards all over the world. One can see that this amount is fixed and coming in, supposedly as payment for some particular product.

Bank officials are also well known for their your business is not my business attitude. That is why they are not going to put up any sort of check on different accounts where **a fixed amount of money** is regularly coming in every day, through credit cards. You and I using a little bit of common sense can immediately sense that there is something wrong with that particular account. Bankers are notoriously blind to any sort of fraudulent malarkey. Why would they want a stop to all that lovely moolah?

That is why when the dispute checking officials finally contact them and ask them about a sum of money coming from my credit card and going into an account in their bank, and the owner of that particular account, the manager of the bank is immediately going to say, no no no no no, we cannot give out this information. Our dear client is going to shut his account with our bank, if he gets to know that you are checking it all the way from India, USA, UK, Philippines, whatever.

And if the dispute checking officials want some more information on the lines of, all right, tell us has this particular owner been getting **regular sums of a fixed amount of money,** from different credit cards, every day, for the past so many months and regularly, the other bankers are going to say with their hands folded in a most superior fashion. "You have no right to ask this information of us. Do you think we are going to give you this information? Our clients have a right to privacy. "

Does not that show very clearly that banks are collaborating with scamsters to encourage Internet fraud?

Credit card divisions are doing the same thing by not blocking stolen cards immediately. I am sorry to say I went online, and looked at the credit card divisions of a number of banks in India. **None of them had an instant card blocking facility online.**

No bank in the world, I think, has the facility to put up an immediate red alert, for accounts in which fixed amounts of money is being transferred from all over the world through credit cards every day. That is because they do not intend to help government agencies trying to prevent Internet and credit card scams.

Their main aim is getting a credit card payment on a credit card, on which they are going to gain 2% or whatever the transaction rate is.

So next time you intend buying a credit card, my suggestion is do not! That is okay, these cards facilitate transactions, especially when you are buying things from abroad, but then with the large number of Internet fraud cases and credit card stealing cases – along with banks who would rather open up investigations and disputes than block cards immediately– why take on another headache.

Banking Secrets Unfolded

Let me tell you one major secret of banking, especially that related to credit cards. I started my career as a banker in Standard Chartered Bank – [taken on later by ANZ Grindlays while I was an employee] way back in the early 90s. I was in the Standard Chartered Gold Card Division. It had just been introduced as a new thing to India.

Later on I would be training bankers in banking techniques, but at that moment, our trainer told us,

"This is a new concept. People like credit cards, because they say, all right, we are going to pay one month from now. So we can buy, buy, buy, until we reach our limit."

Within eight months, I learned how an INR2000 Bill could be stretched to around rupees 3,500, by us bankers.

If you paid up the full amount of rupees 2000, we mentally made faces, even though you were considered to be a good credit card client bet. But we gave you another option. Pay 10% of INR2000 – INR200 – and the rest in installments.

Many of our clients did that. And when they did that, we danced around the room and strew roses out of our hats [figuratively, not literally!]. That is because those clients were caught. Next bill, they would get an amount of 1800 – [2000-200.] With 10.25% added on. And would they want to pay the full amount, or 10% of that?

Many of them paid 10%. And so people not doing the maths did not notice that an INR2000 bill had inflated with interest to around 3500 over a given period of time.

So when I left that job, I promised myself that I would never buy a credit card! Or if I did I would spoil the bankers' day by paying the full amount on the last day of billing through auto debit.

For all those people who do not have credit cards, but want one of them, because banks are telling them that they are a symbol of high status or a desirable thing to have, remember that this is just a marketing stunt. Take that from an ex-banker who has your good at heart. And that is irony, and an oxymoron of the top order.

Nevertheless, we bankers are not your friends. We want your money in any way we can get it. We are going to take it even if we have to hook up with crooks, Internet fraudsters and scamsters. And we are going to block any sort of demand from any legal authority anywhere in the world, demanding to know about the credibility of our clients.

We do not want those clients to stop bringing in all that lovely lolly in our bank accounts. We do not care that it is blood money or illegally obtained money. It is in our hands, and we are not going to be working with either our competition or any other government agency in any decision which removes that money from our vaults.

That is a fact, and you can bank on it.

Once a banker has your money in his hand, he is going to make sure that nobody else gets access to it. That is his marketing promise. Nobody subconsciously includes you, because the last thing he would want you to do is close your account with his bank.

Are there any government agencies which can help in Internet fraud?

As far as I know they are none in Asia. Like I said before, in the USA, you have ic3, which is going to send you a no reply letter and then forget about your complaint.

What is the use of having an antifraud and anticorruption cell when they do not have the resources to check out on frauds?

It is surprising that billions of dollars are being spent by government agencies, in many countries, checking supposedly private Facebook accounts, to see if anything has been posted there pertaining to the political condition of one particular country. After that, these statements are coordinated with the news of that particular day, taken from journals of that country. And so a finger is kept on the pulse of the political state of the world.

There are a number of dedicated geeks who are doing this monitoring job for these agencies. But these DGs would not want to spend some of their time using their cognitive and instincts to recognize financial transactions, taking place regularly in some accounts, which are suspected of belonging to scamsters.

I defy any potential Internet fraudster to protest against his account being frozen. And once an account has been frozen, these geeks could check the credit card number, and reverse the amount back to the bank from where it came.

But no, they will not do it. Their money has not been stolen, has it? Besides, it smacks of too much of hard work.

Bank Update Frauds

How many times have you seen a bank update in your inbox? I get these messages continuously from HDFC and ICICI and American banks, and I do not even have accounts with them now! But they are many of you who do have accounts with them, and may think that there may be a possibility that there is something wrong with your account.

Remember that no bank is going to contact you on the Internet. No bank is going to ask you details which they already have. All they have to do is to switch on the computer and bring up your name. However, Hotmail, Yahoo mail and Gmail are notoriously unreliable, and unsecure sites.

Sending your information, password, credit card details or any other details to be available to any hacker worth his salt is carelessness of the first order. Never download any of these attachments. These are malware and viruses which are going to attack your computer and send all your personal information to these hackers.

I would suggest making sure that all your mail goes into the junk mail or spam mail, from where you delete it as soon as it shows up in your mailbox. Do not download anything, including zip files, and other documents, unless you know the source of origin, which is an address in your in box.

Do not click any button which says click right here to update your information. It is almost as bad as giving your credit card information to someone online.

Here is one of these ICICI bank notices. And I do not even have an account with them. Notice that they do not have my email address? They send it wholesale to recipients. Enjoy the quality of bad English.

Important Notice

Important Notice

Actions

ICICI Bank (update@icicibank.com)

13:59PM

To: Recipients

From: **ICICI Bank** (update@icicibank.com) Your junk email filter is set
to exclusive.

Sent: 26 November 2014 13:59PM

To: Recipients (update@icicibank.com)

Dear Valued Customer,

Please view the attached file for important update.

--Forwarded Message Attachment--

Security Update:

Attn! Dear Customer,

We recently reviewed your account, and suspect that your ICICI Bank
account may have been accessed from an unauthorized computer. This may
be due to changes in your IP address or location. Your account will be
disable within 48 hours, Protecting the security of your account and ICICI
Bank network is our primary concern and that is why your account will be
lock.

To unlock your account please Click the below link to activate and protect your internet banking from internet rat.

www.icicibank.com/new-security/upgrade

**Important Notice:- Please match your information correctly and
carefully to avoid account suspension.**
Thank you for banking with us.

Accounts Management As outlined in our User
Agreement, ICICI � Bank will

periodically send you information about site changes and enhancements.

Visit our Privacy Policy and User Agreement if
you have any questions.

I particularly enjoyed the *Internet rat* bit. You would have been bitten by
real Internet rats, if you had clicked on the URL asking you to upgrade. So
the next time you get this sort of letter asking you to upgrade your
information, which means your name, address, password, and other
particulars, it is almost inviting them to empty out your bank account.

And you know that ICICI bank employees are going to look suitably wide-
eyed and confused when you tell them to block your account and not allow
any transactions to occur. They are going to say, when they finally pick up
the phone, "but did not you give permission for all that money to be
transferred from your account to another account?" With the underlying
emotion of we have other things to do than to keep track of all those people
who want their accounts blocked. Who has the time to type in the account
number and check the status?

Let us open a dispute and put this on to the shoulders of another department
altogether. Careless person, giving his details online to somebody he does
not know. Not our problem. Yes, we know that money has gone to a bank
account in Cyprus, or Spain, or Brazil, but it is the investigation
departments' headache to get that money back. Fat chance.

I would suggest some of these ways in which we can prevent Internet fraud, apart from those already discussed above. Nobody is going to do it, because nobody wants to do anything thought up by somebody else, even though it is going to be very helpful to protect Internet fraud. They also do not like working in tandem with other banks with whom they are competing.

Government agencies unfortunately have made their reputation of being big bullies, taking full advantage of the power invested to them by governments. So naturally they are not going to get any cooperation from bankers, even if they have plenty of polite lip service promising all the cooperation required.

So if these solutions can be tried out globally, they can stop Internet fraud and credit card fraud to a great extent.

Have customer care helplines working properly, including email addresses, and SMSes. Have card blocking facilities online which can be operated by the card owner. If left to the banking authorities and credit card people, a fly-by-night company is going to have ample time to clear up the account, and get away to drink mai tais on a beach in Hawaii for the rest of his life.

In the same way, a credit card owner should be able to flag a particular financial transaction as fraud online, which will immediately block his card and put up a signal against the person demanding money.

This can only be done if any transaction done on a credit card is approved by the credit card holder *before the money goes out of the credit card.*

It is no use you telling me that USD167 have been sent to XYZ and if I approved of the transaction, **after** the transaction had been done on my credit card. By the time I wake up from the shock that my credit card has been used by scamsters, the money has gone out, because nobody bothered to wake up and block the credit card. That was because nobody bothered to check the mail for five days, [9 – 13 November] telling them that a fraud had occurred.

The **before** mail, giving the amount of the money being sent to a customer/client needs to be approved by the owner of the credit card. Unfortunately, as seen in my case there was absolutely no way in which I could contact the bank people after they sent me the approval message because a) – their helpline was not working. b)- their feedback helpline email address was not working and c)- their SMS helpline was not working.

What does a person do under such circumstances? Unfortunately, he is helpless, because he is held to ransom by ineffective and inefficient working of banks all over the world. They could not care less. And then they have the impudence and effrontery to apologize for all the inconvenience caused to us, and whether we would want another new credit card issued!

That is why I am suggesting that the owner of the credit card know how to block his credit card immediately. This should send an auto response message to the bank, as well as to the credit card issuers that there is something fishy about this particular amount of money being demanded by a customer sitting somewhere in Russia, Spain, or in the USA.

The moment he demands the money to be shifted into his account, it should be *Gotcha*. But bankers are never alert. Because they are so busy doing something else. Any problem is going to be put on the shoulders of someone else. And today's work has been done, we will see tomorrow when it comes.

Alternatively, Get people working on **blocking credit cards immediately** and flags going up to the account in which the money has been transferred. Then an international banking network needs to go into part number two – has some other credit card holder somewhere else on earth blocked his card, after a transaction was done on this particular account number? Put a red mark against that account.

Keep track to see if the owner intends to close the account and transfer it somewhere else. That is proof that he is up to no good. You may transfer the account while giving the details of the red flag to the new bank. The new bank officials should be prepared for an investigation in the credibility, credentials and antecedents of that particular account holder.

Every bank asks for identity proofs when opening up a bank account, all over the world. This is the easiest way in which scamsters can be caught. But like I said, who has the energy to do so. Not I.

Conclusion

This book is going to give you plenty of knowledge about Internet frauds, credit card thefts, and how to recognize Internet scams, online and through your email. It also gives practical ways in which Internet fraud can be tackled in a systematic and methodical manner as long as someone is willing to take on the responsibility of tracking down scamsters with the active cooperation of banks all over the world.

So do not ever make yourself open to Internet fraud or credit card identity theft. Read the tips and techniques given in this book, and follow them. A little bit of prevention today is going to be worth hours of heartache saved and a tension free existence.

Author Bio-

Dueep Jyot Singh is a Management and IT Professional who managed to gather Postgraduate qualifications in Management and English and Degrees in Science, French and Education while pursuing different enjoyable career options like being an hospital administrator, IT,SEO and HRD Database Manager/ trainer, movie , radio and TV scriptwriter, theatre artiste and public speaker, lecturer in French, Marketing and Advertising, ex-Editor of Hearts On Fire (now known as Solstice) Books Missouri USA, advice columnist and cartoonist, publisher and Aviation School trainer, ex-moderator on Medico.in, banker, student councilor ,travelogue writer ... among other things!

One fine morning, she decided that she had enough of killing herself by Degrees and went back to her first love -- writing. It's more enjoyable! She already has 48 published academic and 14 fiction- in- different- genre books under her belt.

When she is not designing websites or making Graphic design illustrations for clients , she is browsing through old bookshops hunting for treasures, of which she has an enviable collection – including R.L. Stevenson, O.Henry, Dornford Yates, Maurice Walsh, De Maupassant, Victor Hugo, Sapper, C.N. Williamson, "Bartimeus" and the crown of her collection- Dickens "The Old Curiosity Shop," and so on... Just call her "Renaissance Woman") - collecting herbal remedies, acting like Universal Helping Hand/Agony Aunt, or escaping to her dear mountains for a bit of exploring, collecting herbs and plants and trekking.

Our books are available at
1. Amazon.com
2. Barnes and Noble
3. Itunes
4. Kobo
5. Smashwords
6. Google Play Books

Check out some of the other JD-Biz Publishing books

Gardening Series on Amazon

Health Learning Series

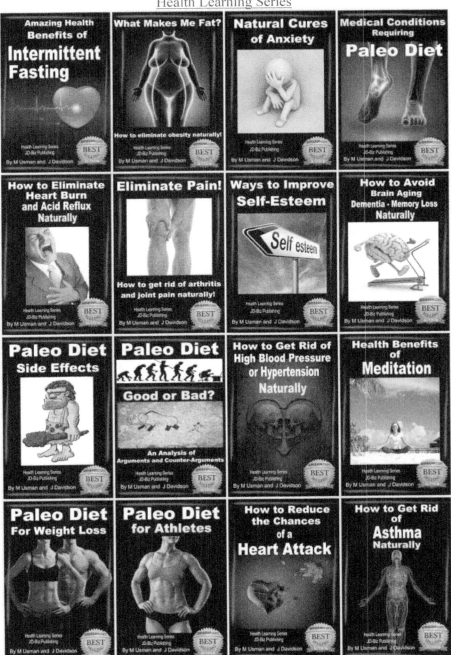

Learn To Draw Series

How to Build and Plan Books

Entrepreneur Book Series

Publisher

JD-Biz Corp

P O Box 374

Mendon, Utah 84325

http://www.jd-biz.com/

Printed in Great Britain
by Amazon

48845670R00050